Discovering
Machu Picchu

By Linda Cernak

Scott Foresman
is an imprint of

Glenview, Illinois • Boston, Massachusetts • Chandler, Arizona • Upper Saddle River, New Jersey

Illustrations

3, 4, 8 Judith Hunt.

Photographs

Every effort has been made to secure permission and provide appropriate credit for photographic material. The publisher deeply regrets any omission and pledges to correct errors called to its attention in subsequent editions.

Unless otherwise acknowledged, all photographs are the property of Pearson Education, Inc.

Photo locators denoted as follows: Top (T), Center (C), Bottom (B), Left (L), Right (R), Background (Bkgd)

1 ©DK Images; **6** ©The Granger Collection, NY; **7** ©The Granger Collection, NY; **11** (CR) ©DK Images, (TL) ©Stockxpert; **12** ©Mitch Diamond/Index Stock Imagery/ PhotoLibrary Group, Inc..

ISBN 13: 978-0-328-46920-8
ISBN 10:   0-328-46920-3

3 4 5 6 7 8 9 10 V010 13 12 11 10

The Inca lived hundreds of years ago. They lived in what is now Peru, in South America. They lived in the high mountains They built cities and roads. But their way of life died out.

Over time, trees grew on the mountains. Vines grew over the stones. Rain washed out the roads. People forgot about the Inca city.

The buildings became ruins. Ruins are what's left of very old buildings.

Hundreds of years later, Hiram Bingham came to Peru. He heard stories of a lost city. It was high in the mountains. But no one was sure where it was.

Bingham was sure he could find it. He met some farmers who told him about old stones and paths. A young boy said he knew where to go. The boy led Hiram through the forest.

They crossed fast rivers. They went through thick brush. They climbed up steep paths.

At last, the boy pointed at something ahead. At first, Bingham couldn't see anything. Then he looked through the thick vines.

Bingham couldn't believe his eyes! He saw huge stones and stairways. He saw hundreds of ruins. He saw hillsides where people had grown food 400 years ago.

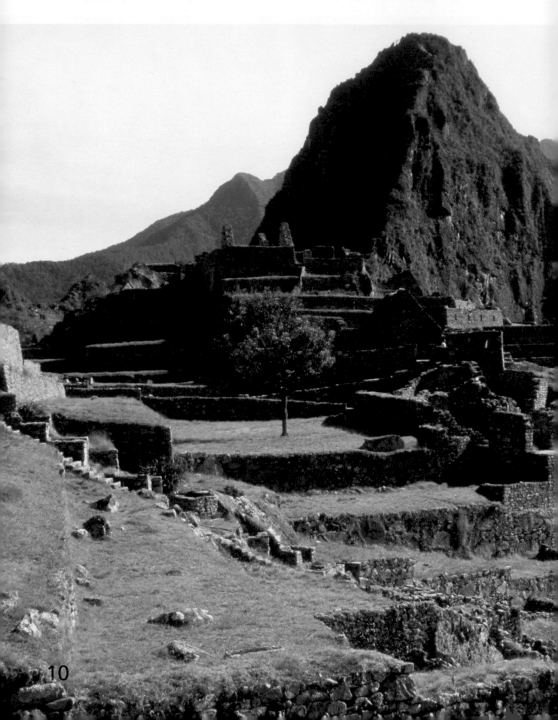

Bingham had found the "lost" city of Machu Picchu!

Bingham's trip was full of wonderful surprises. But the best surprise of all was finding Machu Picchu.

Today, people from all over the world come to Machu Picchu as tourists. They love to visit the ruins that are there.